CONTENTS

WALKER BOOKS
AND SUBSIDIARIES
LONDON · BOSTON · SYDNEY

ROCKING AND ROLLING

Philip Steele

LINCOLNSHIRE   JSSO

1 There are volcanoes all over the world. Scientists who study them are called vulcanologists, and they try to work out when volcanoes are going to erupt.

2 Sometimes the scientists climb down into the mouth of a volcano to check what's going on.

3 When they do this, they have to wear special clothing to protect them from the heat and the poisonous gases that a volcano gives off.

4 They use a machine called a seismometer to measure the ground shaking, and a special thermometer to take the temperature inside the volcano. This information helps the vulcanologists tell how close the volcano is to erupting.

5 When it gets too dangerous for people to go inside the volcano, a robot is sent down instead. It can do many of the same jobs as the scientists, and it doesn't have to wear any special clothing!

2 VOLCANOES

BLOWING ITS TOP!

1 This is a very strange-looking mountain. What's happened to the top of it? There's just a big hole where its peak should be.

2 The hole is called a crater, and it tells us that the mountain is a volcano.

3 And now this volcano is erupting! Clouds of smoke and grey ash are billowing out, filling the air with stinking, poisonous gases.

4 Boiling rivers of red-hot rock are gushing out of the crater and streaming down the sides of the volcano. The rock is called lava, and it comes from deep under the ground.

5 Far beneath the volcano there's a great hollow. It's called a chamber, and it's a place where gases and hot gooey rock called magma collect.

4 VOLCANOES

6 When a volcano erupts, it's because the gases and magma are forcing their way up through giant cracks in the ground and out through the crater.

Crater

Volcano

Chamber

7 And when magma reaches the Earth's surface, we call it lava.

8 Eventually the volcano stops erupting. The lava cools and hardens into black rock, and the mountain is quiet — until the next time!

LAND AHOY

1 Sparkling blue seawater laps gently at the shores of a beautiful island. Long sandy beaches stretch as far as the eye can see...

2 ...but wait a minute. Why is the sand black? And look at the crater on **top** of that mountain.

3 Well, the colour of the sand tells us what it's made from — black volcanic lava. And that crater shows that the island is really just the tip of a huge volcano.

6 VOLCANIC ISLANDS

4 The island began forming long long ago, when magma burst up through a crack in the seabed.

5 As the hot gooey magma met the cold seawater, it hardened into shiny black rock.

6 Eruption followed eruption, and the rock slowly grew into a mountain. Then one day, its top broke through the surface of the sea — our island had been born!

1 In 1963, some fishermen were sailing off the coast of Iceland when suddenly they spotted a huge cloud of steam billowing up from the waves.

2 The fishermen watched in astonishment as a mound of black steaming rock heaved up from the sea like a huge whale. What was going on?

3 Over the years, a volcanic island had been forming under the water, and now it had grown so high that its top was breaking through the surface.

4 Today, the island is the size of a small city. It's called Surtsey, which means Devil Island in Icelandic — one reason, perhaps, why no one lives there!

VOLCANIC ISLANDS 7

1 Hot springs are pools or streams of naturally hot water. They're found where rain water has collected underground, and been heated by hot rocks deep inside the Earth.

1 Whoooosh! A great fountain-like jet of hot water and steam spurts up out of the ground. This is a geyser.

2 People all over the world make use of underground hot water. In Iceland, the water is piped into peoples' homes to provide heating.

2 The water and steam are coming from the underground pools that form when rain seeps down through cracks in the rocks.

3 In Budapest, in Hungary, the water from hot springs is fed into open-air swimming pools.

4

But people aren't the only ones who like warm water. There are hot springs high in the snowy mountains of Japan, where monkeys called macaques go swimming!

8 SPRINGS

FULL STEAM AHEAD

3 The deeper you go into the Earth, the hotter it gets. And when an underground pool gets hot enough, the water boils and turns into steam.

4 The steam then forces its way back through the rocks, pushing any water in the cracks up in front of it — and blasting out into the air as a geyser.

5 The world's tallest geyser is in Yellowstone National Park, in the United States. It's called the Steamboat, and it can shoot to the amazing height of 100 metres!

DOWN UNDER

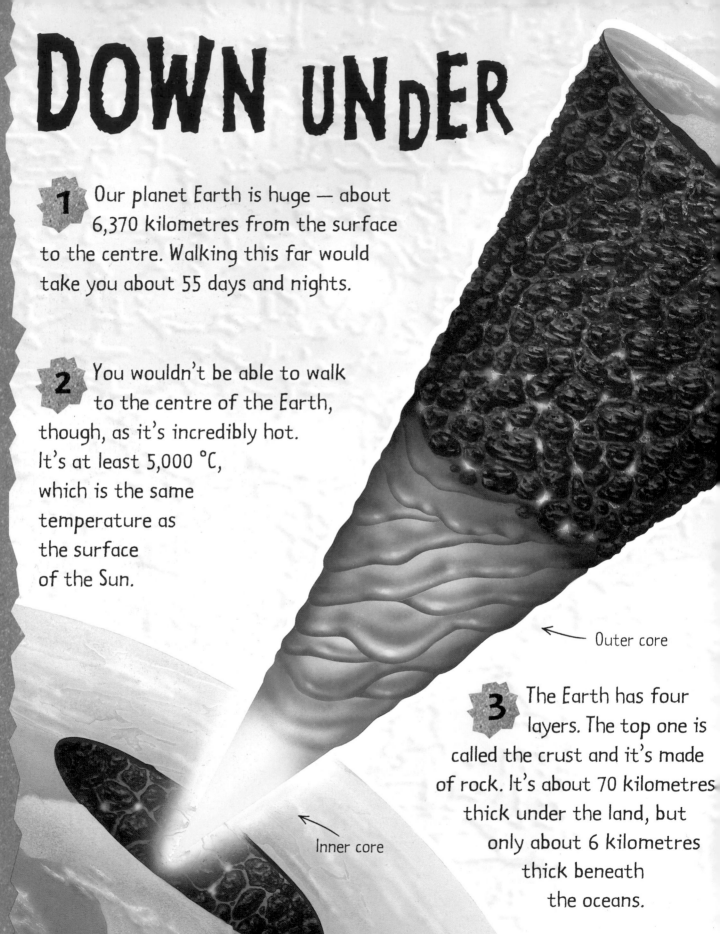

1 Our planet Earth is huge — about 6,370 kilometres from the surface to the centre. Walking this far would take you about 55 days and nights.

2 You wouldn't be able to walk to the centre of the Earth, though, as it's incredibly hot. It's at least 5,000 °C, which is the same temperature as the surface of the Sun.

Outer core

Inner core

3 The Earth has four layers. The top one is called the crust and it's made of rock. It's about 70 kilometres thick under the land, but only about 6 kilometres thick beneath the oceans.

10

4 The mantle is next. It's also made of rock, but it's so hot that parts have melted into magma and are as gooey as porridge.

Crust ←

Mantle ←

5 Beneath the mantle is the Earth's core. This is made of metal and has two layers — an outer and an inner core.

6 The outer core is runny because it's so hot. But although the inner core is even hotter, it's solid. Why? Because the other three layers are pressing down on it, and the weight is enough to squash it solid!

1 People have always dreamed of digging down to the Earth's centre. But so far no one has invented a machine that would survive the heat.

2 The world's deepest mineshaft is in Carletonville, South Africa. But even at 3.5 kilometres deep, it's little more than a pinprick in the Earth's crust.

3 The deepest a person has ever been is the Mariana Trench, a crack in the Pacific Ocean floor. In 1960, a two-man sub dived down into the trench — nearly 11 kilometres below the sea's surface.

4 In 1970, Russian scientists began drilling a hole into the Earth's crust. By 1992, they'd dug more than 12 kilometres down. The temperature at the bottom was over 200 °C — yet the hole was still nowhere near the mantle layer!

INSIDE THE EARTH 11

1 The Earth didn't always look like it does today. Once upon a time there was just one vast landmass, called Pangaea.

200 million years ago

2 Very very slowly, as the Earth's plates drifted on the mantle layer, Pangaea began to break up.

100 million years ago

3 As Pangaea gradually split apart, the Earth's seven great landmasses, the continents, formed.

The Earth today

4 The Earth's plates are still drifting, so this is what scientists think our planet will look like in the future.

50 million years' time

1 If all the oceans disappeared, the Earth would look just like a jigsaw made up of lots of big pieces.

2 The pieces are called plates, and there are about 20 of them. They float on the Earth's mantle, moving very very slowly — between 2 and 20 centimetres a year.

3 Sometimes the plates move apart, and gooey magma rises up from the mantle to fill the gap. The magma cools and hardens to form new land or ocean floor.

12 PLATE MOVEMENT

CRACKING UP

4 Sometimes two plates push against each other. The edge of one plate may slide under the other and melt back to magma...

5 ...or the two plate edges may crumple up into a range of mountains — even below the oceans.

QUAKE AND SHAKE

1 Just a few minutes ago this truck was speeding along the road. Then, suddenly, there was a terrifying roar and the ground opened up — an earthquake!

2 The most serious earthquakes happen deep underground, along the edges of the Earth's plates.

3 Usually, the plates stay jammed close together. But from time to time, a plate breaks away.

4 This makes the ground shudder and shake. Sometimes, it can even split wide open.

14 EARTHQUAKES

5 The shudders can be felt thousands of kilometres away, because they spread out from the earthquake's centre like the ripples from a stone thrown into a pond.

6 Every year, there are 40,000 to 50,000 earthquakes which are strong enough to be felt. Fortunately, only about 40 of them are big enough to cause any damage.

1 It's fairly easy for scientists to tell where most earthquakes will take place, but hard to work out when. So people in high-risk areas such as Japan and the west coast of the United States must always be prepared.

2 Architects try to design buildings that will stand up to the ground shaking. For example, the Trans-America building in San Francisco is a slender pyramid because this is such a sturdy shape.

3 In Japan there's a National Disaster Prevention Day each year, when everyone practises what to do during an earthquake. Volunteers spend the day learning how to rescue people from fallen buildings.

4 And in the American state of California, children have earthquake drills at school. One thing they're taught is to shelter under their desks — it's the safest place to be if the roof falls in.

1 The town of Port Royal is on the island of Jamaica, in the Caribbean Sea. In the 1660s, it was a base for pirates from all over the world.

Port Royal

2 But on 7 June 1692, Port Royal was hit by a massive earthquake. The ground shook violently up and down, and many of the town's houses collapsed.

3 Then a huge wall of water, a tsunami, rolled in from the ocean, lifting up sailing ships and smashing them like matchwood. The wave killed more than 2,000 people.

4 In those days, people knew very little about what makes earthquakes and tsunamis happen. The islanders thought that the giant wave had been sent to punish the pirates for being so wicked!

1 Most waves are made by the wind blowing over the sea. This is no ordinary wave, though. It's called a tsunami, and it was started by an earthquake.

16 TSUNAMIS

WALLS OF WATER

2 A big earthquake is rather like a huge bomb going off. The force of the explosion can create a tsunami that travels thousands of kilometres through the ocean.

3 When the tsunami is in deep ocean water, its top may only be 20–30 centimetres above the surface.

4 But as it rolls on into shallower water near the coast, the tsunami is forced upwards into a gigantic wall of water — sometimes it can be even higher than a block of flats!

HIGHER AND HIGHER

1 Welcome to the top of the world. The Himalayas are the highest mountain ranges on Earth, and the tallest Himalayan peak is Mount Everest.

2 Everest already soars to a height of 8,848 metres. But next year it will be a tiny bit higher — it's still growing.

1 Long ago, people made up stories to explain where mountains came from. In one tale they were elephants that had been magically turned into stone. But, of course, mountains are really made by the rocking and rolling movements of the Earth's crust.

2 There are three main kinds of mountain. Fold mountains, like the Himalayas, form when the Earth's plates crunch into each other, and layers of the crust are pushed up into loops and bumps.

3 The Himalayas started forming about 53 million years ago, when the Earth's plate carrying the land that is now India began crunching upwards into the rest of Asia.

4 Centimetre by centimetre, India pushed northwards. And over tens of millions of years, the plate edges crumpled into the huge ridges, peaks and valleys we see today.

Himalayas

Everest

CHINA

INDIA

3 Block mountains are made when part of the crust is forced up between two cracks in a plate. These cracks are called faults.

4 Dome mountains happen when magma bulges up beneath the crust. This forces the crust up into a large rounded hump — rather like the back of an elephant!

1 High in the highest mountains, it's so cold that snow doesn't melt, even in summer. As more snow falls, it packs down hard into hollows and the snow turns to ice.

2 When a hollow is full, the ice slides down the mountain as a glacier. Most glaciers move very slowly — the fastest creep less than a metre a day.

Glacier

3 Pieces of loose rock are frozen into the bottom of the glacier, and as it edges along they scrape at the ground underneath. Over the ages, this gritty ice grinds the land away, leaving a deep valley.

4 A valley made by a glacier is a very different shape to one made by a river. This valley was worn away by a river. The fast-flowing water cut through the land making a shape like a V.

5 This valley was carved out by a glacier. The ice was much slower than the river and, like a great bulldozer, the glacier cut out a U-shape from the rock.

20 GLACIERS

GOING, GOING, GONE!

1 It took hundreds of thousands of years to make this enormous valley. But although it happened so long ago, we know what did the work.

2 A mighty river once flowed here. And like all rivers, it carried grit and pebbles that rubbed against the land, slowly wearing it away and carving out a valley.

3 The river has long since dried up and disappeared. But look what it's left behind.

4 How come these strange pillars of rock are here? Why didn't the river wear them away?

5 Well, some rocks are harder than others, and hard rocks break down more slowly than soft ones. The river dried up before it had time to wear these pillars away.

6 The wearing away of the land is called erosion, and it's still going on today. But water isn't doing the work now — so what is?

22 EROSION

7 The answer is blowing in the wind. Day after day it whistles through the valley, picking up grit and sand, and blasting everything it touches.

8 It works like sandpaper, slowly wearing the rocks down and grinding them into weird and wonderful shapes.

9 Rocks are so much harder than wind and water — yet in time, both are powerful enough to shape the land we live on.

INDEX

Main illustrations by Chris Forsey (cover, 3, 4-5, 8-9); Christian Hook (16-17);
Ian Jackson (20-23); Mike Lister (14-15); Darren Pattenden (18-19); Luis Rey (12-13);
Ian Thompson (10-11); Peter Visscher (6-7).
Inset and picture-strip illustrations by Ian Thompson.

Designed by Jonathan Hair and Matthew Lilly, edited by Sarah Hudson.

Consultant: Keith Lye

First published 1997 by Walker Books Ltd, 87 Vauxhall Walk, London SE11 5HJ

This edition published 1998

2 4 6 8 10 9 7 5 3

Text © 1997 Philip Steele
Illustrations © 1997 Walker Books Ltd

This book has been typeset in Kosmik.

Printed in Hong Kong

British Library Cataloguing in Publication Data
A catalogue record for this book is available from the British Library.

ISBN 0-7445-6063-2

QUIZ ANSWERS

Page 2 — TRUE

Mars and Venus both have volcanoes.
The biggest is 26 kilometres high. It's on
Mars and it's called Olympus Mons.

Page 6 — FALSE

The island of Pulau Batu Hairan, off the
coast of Malaysia, appeared in 1988.

Page 9 — FALSE

Using information about when a geyser has
erupted in the past, scientists can work out
when it's likely to blow its top again.

Page 10 — TRUE

The Earth's core and the Moon are both
about 3,500 kilometres thick, measured
straight across the middle.

Page 13 — FALSE

They are moving apart at a rate of
about 2-3 centimetres a year.

Page 14 — FALSE

Usually, earthquakes last for something
between a few seconds and a minute.

Page 17 — TRUE

Tsunamis can travel at over 900 kilometres
per hour — as fast as a jet plane.

Page 19 — TRUE

The Hawaiian volcano, Mauna Kea, rises
10,205 metres from the sea bed, but only
the top 4,205 metres are above the water.
Everest is 8,848 metres above sea level.

Page 20 — FALSE

Some valleys are formed by movements
of the Earth's crust.